Excelling With Data
Descriptive Statistics Using Microsoft® Excel

Keith Resendes

Copyright

Disclaimer

Trademarks

ISBN-13: 978-1491029121
ISBN-10: 1491029129

Contents

Preface

Learning statistics may be a challenge. Maybe using MS Excel to analyze data is a challenge. Either way, this book is intended for those who would like to learn statistics and/or Excel. This book will come in handy if you are taking a social science class, a statistics class, or even if you just want to learn the techniques used in this book for your job. It can serve many purposes depending on your needs. This is the first book of a multi-series for instruction.

I have written this book with you in mind either as a student or an employee trying to gain more knowledge or refresh your skills. I have made the explanations as clear as possible for the ease of learning statistics and Excel. Encouragement has been provided throughout and I believe anyone can use this book even if you don't have much knowledge in either statistics or Excel. I have only explained the most popular techniques to which are used in the working fields or school courses. Such techniques include basic statistics, e.g. averages, standard deviations; pivot tables, histograms and data retrieval. There are far more explanations and in-depth discussion of statistics and Excel but have been omitted for the shortness of this book, as well as promoting only the most common topics.

I hope you gain a lot out of this book and stay motivated to learn more. As a student, I have looked for the right book to help me with subjects that I had a difficult time understanding. Sometimes the resources I had been looking through were not as clear in explanation, and examples lacked clarification or were not present. It is recommended that you read the book clearly and follow the instructions precisely and I truly believe you will be able to complete all of the exercises. I believe that anyone can learn anything as long as they put their mind and effort to it.

Acknowledgements

I would like to express my gratitude by thanking my professor and mentor Dr. Gary Davis for inspiring and encouraging me to write this book. For my mother who has provided mention of writing on a weekly basis, and her nonstop support. I would also like to thank my peers for their support as well.

Chapter 1

Mean, Median, Mode

So you want to analyze data? The first things to do are open up Excel and view your blank sheet. If you already haven't done so, collect your data you want to analyze. It is very important that you gather your data and keep it organized. What do I mean by this? It is imperative that the data stay organized and are under their corresponding headings. For instance, say you want to analyze the average weight of animals in a zoo. You have records for three types of mammals; orangutans, chimpanzees, and spider monkeys. You also have recorded weights for ten orangutans, ten chimpanzees, and ten spider monkeys. So to have organized data means not to be careless with values from orangutans and mix them up with chimps or spider monkeys. See Table 1 below.

Orangutans	Chimpanzees	Spider Monkeys
155	112	16
144	127	13
145	115	13
140	121	17
142	126	15
152	123	17
147	119	17
146	122	13
139	124	15
141	121	18

Now that we are clear on organized data, let's go ahead and enter these values into Excel. The table below represents your log of recorded weights for these three mammals. Here's how it will look in Excel.

Figure 1.1: Table with recorded data

	A	B	C	D
1	Orangutans	Chimpanzees	Spider Monkeys	
2	155	112	16	
3	144	127	13	
4	145	115	13	
5	140	121	17	
6	142	126	15	
7	152	123	17	
8	147	119	17	
9	146	122	13	
10	139	124	15	
11	141	121	18	
12				

You may want to format the cells for a more professional look by centering the headers of each column or maybe left-aligning the values of weights. You are free to do whatever you feel most comfortable doing.

Figure 1.2: Table with formatted cells

	A	B	C	D
	E8		f_x	
1	Orangutans	Chimpanzees	Spider Monkeys	
2	155	112	16	
3	144	127	13	
4	145	115	13	
5	140	121	17	
6	142	126	15	
7	152	123	17	
8	147	119	17	
9	146	122	13	
10	139	124	15	
11	141	121	18	
12				
13				
14				

1.1 Mean

You now entered your data and want to do some analysis, basic descriptive analysis. Why don't we start off with the average? What is the average? By mathematical definition it is represented as

$$\bar{x} = \frac{\text{sum of the quantities}}{\text{number of items}}.$$

That is, in this case, say for average weight of orangutans, the calculation would look like this:

$$\bar{x} = \frac{155 + 144 + 145 + 140 + 142 + 152 + 147 + 146 + 139 + 141}{10}$$

$$= \frac{1451}{10}$$

$$= 145.1 \text{lbs.}$$

Therefore, the average for the orangutans is 145.1 pounds. Average is also called the mean.

Excel can easily calculate the mean, or average, of any column or row as long as they are numeric. Let's go ahead and calculate the averages for orangutans, chimpanzees, and spider monkeys.

First, highlight the 10 values of weights for the orangutans. Then look for the $\sum$ button located on the top-right menu bar in Excel. Click on the drop-down arrow and select **Average**. Do the same for the remaining mammals as I did (Figure 1.4).

Figure 1.3: Highlighted data values

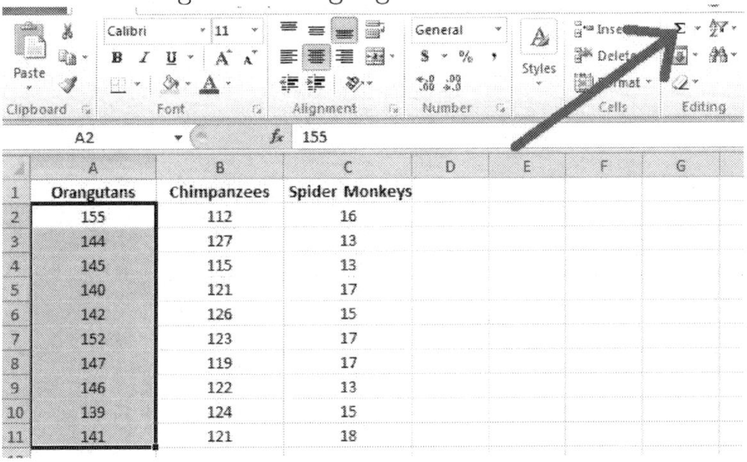

Now you should have something like this:

Figure 1.4: Calculated means for orangutans, chimpanzees, and spider monkeys

	Clipboard		Font		Alignment		Num
	G13	▾		f_x			
◢	A		B		C		I
1	Orangutans		Chimpanzees		Spider Monkeys		
2	155		112		16		
3	144		127		13		
4	145		115		13		
5	140		121		17		
6	142		126		15		
7	152		123		17		
8	147		119		17		
9	146		122		13		
10	139		124		15		
11	141		121		18		
12		145.1		121		15.4	
13							

1.2 Median

Sometimes data does not sit close to the mean. For example, real estate is a very skewed distribution: if you were to look at house prices in any given neighborhood you would notice that it is skewed. Suppose a few very highly priced houses were listed in a particular neighborhood and the others were relatively low, then these houses would pull up the average house price so that it is no longer typical. Similarly, if Shaquille O'Neil walked into a classroom of young children the average heights rises significantly. In these cases, we need another indication of the rough center of the data - the *median*.

Why do we want to calculate the median? For one, in many cases, such as height and weight of people, or animals, the data concentrates close to the mean. In the case of the house prices the mean could be high due to one house having a higher value than the rest, so we use the median.

Let us now calculate the median. The median is the number which is in the middle, hence the term "median". The numbers in the set must first be arranged from smallest to biggest. If the number of items in the set are odd then it is quite easy to get the median, say the set is 4, 11, 17, 19, 25, then median number is simply 17. If the set has an even number of items as in 4, 11, 17, 19, 25, 26, then the median is 18. Wait! How did I get that number? Since there is an even number of items in this set we must take the middle *two* numbers, 17 and 19, add them up and divide by 2.

$$\frac{17 + 19}{2} = 18$$

Look familiar? Yes! It is the average between two numbers. Of course, if you have a large data set you would want to use Excel to calculate the median.

Using a similar command as **AVERAGE** you can just as easily calculate the median. Click the cell below the average value for orangutans and type in **=MEDIAN**. Excel will automatically show you what you need to input. It would show something like **MEDIAN(number1,[number2],...)**.

Next, highlight the ten values for orangutans and close the argument (the stuff inside the parentheses) with a parenthesis. If you don't there will get an error. See Figure 1.5.

Figure 1.5: Calculating the median

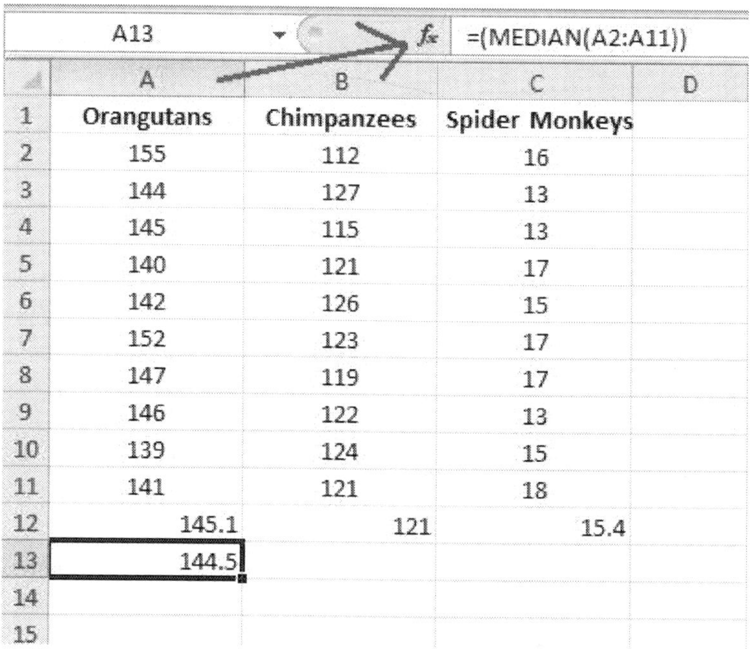

	A	B	C	D
	A13	▾	f_x =(MEDIAN(A2:A11))	
1	Orangutans	Chimpanzees	Spider Monkeys	
2	155	112	16	
3	144	127	13	
4	145	115	13	
5	140	121	17	
6	142	126	15	
7	152	123	17	
8	147	119	17	
9	146	122	13	
10	139	124	15	
11	141	121	18	
12	145.1	121	15.4	
13	144.5			
14				
15				

Notice we did not need to sort the values in the column. Excel has done that internally and calculated the median. Moving forward, I obtained the median for the other mammals. You should get something like this:

Figure 1.6: Calculated medians for orangutans, chimpanzees, and spider monkeys

	A	B	C	D
1	Orangutans	Chimpanzees	Spider Monkeys	
2	155	112	16	
3	144	127	13	
4	145	115	13	
5	140	121	17	
6	142	126	15	
7	152	123	17	
8	147	119	17	
9	146	122	13	
10	139	124	15	
11	141	121	18	
12	145.1	121	15.4	
13	144.5	121.5	15.5	
14				
15				

So you know, when entering a function in Excel, i.e. addition, subtraction, multiplication, division, median, etc., you must first enter "=". This tells Excel that you are entering a function. Even **AVERAGE** is a function. But because **AVERAGE** is very common Excel has it built in under the drop-down menu pointed out earlier and so you did not need to do this (although you still can).

1.3   Mode

What is mode? The mode is the item in a set that shows up most often. If you have a set of 100 numbers and the number 7 shows up, say 11 times then so it occurs more often than any other numbers with fewer occurrences and is so called the Mode. If you go to a bake shop and see that the glazed doughnuts have more quantity than the chocolate frosted and the other types of doughnuts then that means that the mode for the set of doughnuts is the glazed doughnut. Let's take a look at the mammals example again. Enter =**MODE** in the cell below the median for orangutans and highlight the ten values and follow by closing the argument. What do you get? Right! Excel executes #**N/A**. If you notice in this set there are no items or values that repeat more than the next. So there is no mode. I went ahead and did the last two.

Figure 1.7: Calculated modes for orangutans, chimpanzees, and spider monkeys

	A	B	C	
1	Orangutans	Chimpanzees	Spider Monkeys	
2	155	112	16	
3	144	127	13	
4	145	115	13	
5	140	121	17	
6	142	126	15	
7	152	123	17	
8	147	119	17	
9	146	122	13	
10	139	124	15	
11	141	121	18	
12	145.1	121	15.4	
13	144.5	121.5	15.5	
14	#N/A	121	13	
15				

What happened to the mode in the Spider Monkeys column? If you look closely there are actually two modes, 13 and 17. So why did Excel execute only 13? That is because it was the first mode to appear. To get the second, third, etc. you need to do the following. The data is in the range C2:C11. Enter the formula =**MODE(C2:C11)** in C15. This will return the 1st mode. Next, enter this array formula

```
=MODE(IF(COUNTIF(C$2:C2,C$2:C$11)=0,C$2:C$11))
```

in C15. Array formulas need to be entered using the key combination CTRL+SHIFT+ENTER, not just ENTER. Hold down the CTRL key, the SHIFT key, and then the ENTER key. You will see 13 appear again. In that cell with the new 13 copy down until you get #N/A errors. You will need to hover the mouse pointer over the cell's bottom-right corner until you see a bold cross appear. Click that bold cross and hold and drag down until you see the error. You should see 13, 13, 17, 17, 15, #N/A, #N/A. Great! You are on a roll! Check your work with mine in Figure 1.8.

Figure 1.8: Calculated modes for orangutans, chimpanzees, and spider monkeys

	A	B	C	D	E
1	Orangutans	Chimpanzees	Spider Monkeys		
2	155	112	16		
3	144	127	13		
4	145	115	13		
5	140	121	17		
6	142	126	15		
7	152	123	17		
8	147	119	17		
9	146	122	13		
10	139	124	15		
11	141	121	18		
12	145.1	121	15.4		
13	144.5	121.5	15.5		
14	#N/A	121	13		
15			13		
16			17		
17			17		
18			15		
19			#N/A		
20			#N/A		

Try an exercise on your own. If you don't have data you can get data from `histogramma.com` under **Data** titled **MMM**. Using this data, try to calculate the mean, median, and mode. Answers: Mean = 5.5, Median = 6, Mode = 6,8,10.

Mean:

- Highlight all the values in the column.

- Click the $\sum$ button located on the top-right menu bar.

- Select **Average**.

Median:

- Click on a blank cell and type in **=MEDIAN**.

- Highlight all the values in the column.

Mode:

- Click on a blank cell and type in **=MODE**.

- Highlight all the values in the column.

More than one mode? Test it.

- Click on a blank cell and enter

  `=MODE(IF(COUNTIF()=0,))`

  where (IF(COUNTIF()=0,)) contains data range. If the range is, for example, A1:A560 then enter

  `A$1:A1,A$1:A$560`

  in the COUNTIF parenthesis. It would look like

  `(IF(COUNTIF(A$1:A1,A$1:A$560)=0,))`

- Enter the cell range again after the "," to complete the argument. It would look like

  `(IF(COUNTIF(A$1:A1,A$1:A$560)=0,A$1:A$560))`

- Use key combination CTRL+SHIFT+ENTER. Remember, this is an array formula.

- Lastly, you will see one number appear, so you will need to click that cell, then hover over the bottom-right of that cell until the mouse cursor changes to a bold cross, then click and drag until you see **#N/A**.

Chapter 2

How To Make A Histogram

Now that you know the basics of entering data into an Excel spreadsheet, calculate the mean, median and mode you should now be ready to produce a histogram. A histogram is a type of graph that has wide applications in statistics. They allow a visual interpretation of data by indicating the number of data points that lie within a range of values, usually called a bin. The bars represent the frequency of the data that lie within each bin. Take a look at the typical histogram shown below. This is a distribution of data on percent of diabetic individuals in U.S. counties in 2008. I will show you how to make a histogram using MS Excel.

Figure 2.1: Distribution of diabetic patients, 2008

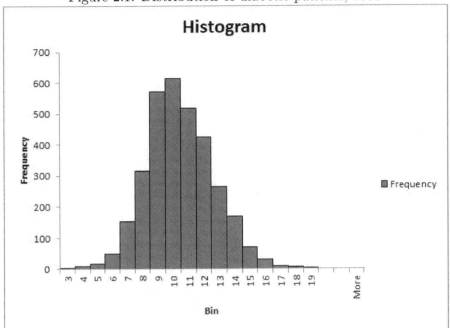

This data can be extracted from my website `histogramma.com` under **Data** titled **Diabetes 2008**. Open this file up and save it to your computer.

Before we can go ahead and plot a histogram with this data we should first take sight of the maximum and minimum values of the data set. This is important so that you can estimate how wide you want your bin to be. For this exercise I have chosen bin sizes of 1. The data has accuracy to one decimal place, e.g. 12.8, 14.3. In C2, enter the maximum value of the data set and in C3 enter the minimum value. This is done by typing **=MAX(A2:A3220)** in C2, or by selecting all the data in column A but not including the header "Percent", and **=MIN(A2:A3220)** in C3 respectively. Choosing the bin size is entirely up to you, however, if the bins are too wide then you risk not visualizing what is going on with the data. If the bin size is too small then again you cannot really see what is going on. Try it! Use different bin sizes for your histogram. So in B2 through B18 enter 3 up to 19. This will be the bin size.

Now go to the **Data** tab in Excel and click the **Data Analysis** button at the top-right corner.

Figure 2.2: Click Data tab

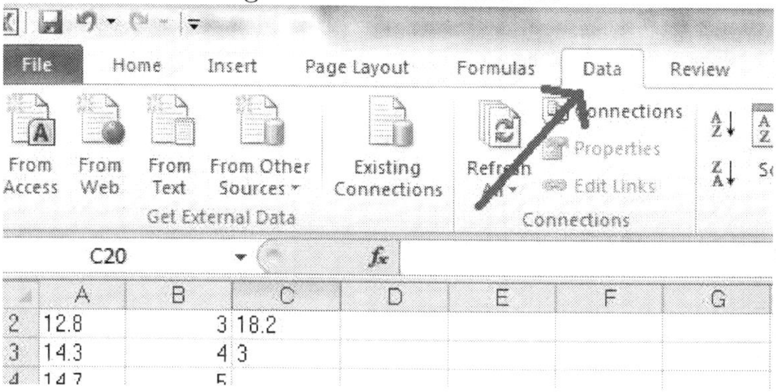

Figure 2.3: Click Data Analysis

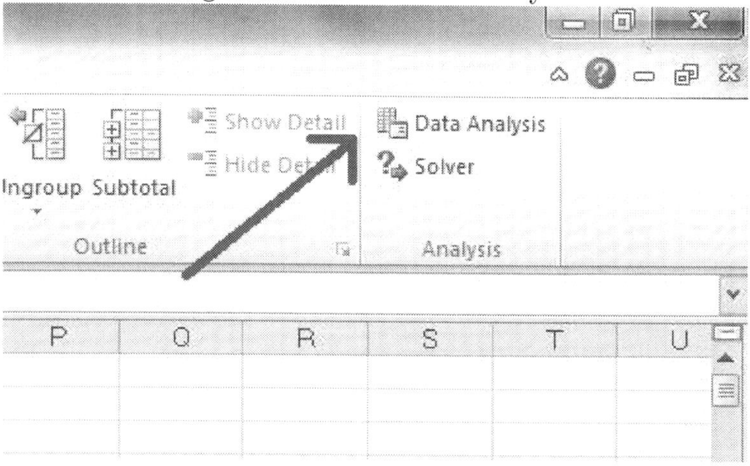

Look for **Histogram** and click **OK**. In the **Input Range** text box enter **A2:A3220** or select the cells using the mouse. Next, in the **Bin Range** text box, select the cells from the bin range column. You also may want to select **Chart Output**. Click **OK** when done. See Figures 2.4 and 2.5.

Figure 2.4: Click Histogram

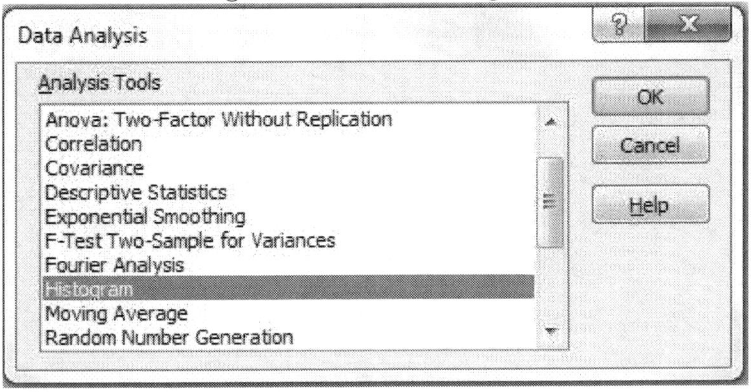

Figure 2.5: Enter information

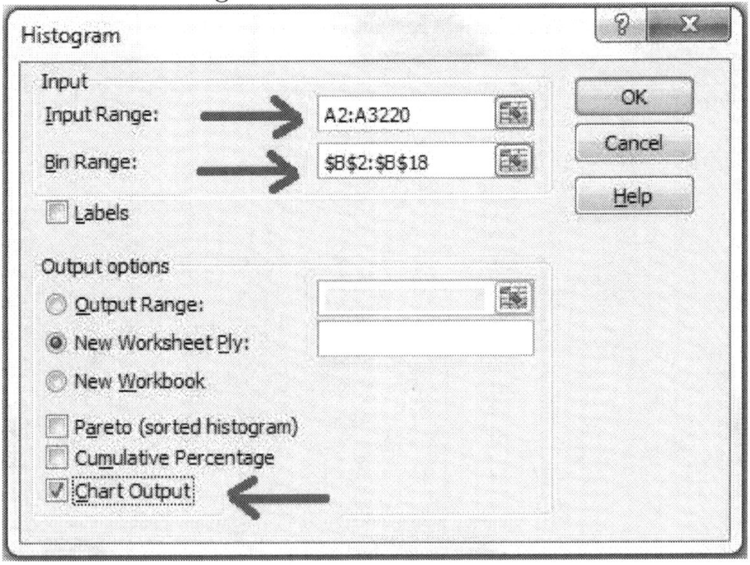

You should now have a histogram. Verify that you have a histogram as in Figure 2.6.

Figure 2.6: Complete histogram

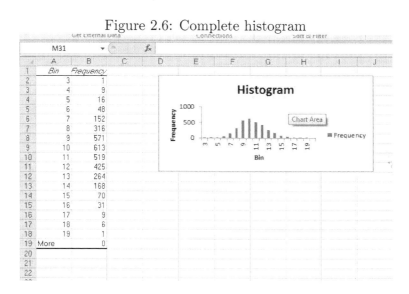

The histogram doesn't look much like the histograms we normally see. There are gaps between each bar. This can easily be fixed by right-clicking on one of the blue data series bars then selecting **Format Data Series**. A dialogue box will appear. Select **Series Options**, if not already selected. Now toggle the slide button to the left for less gap or to the right for greater gap. This exercise uses no gap. Refer to Figures 2.7-2.8.

Next, to add a border with color, select **Border Color**, **Solid line**, and then **Color**. Refer to Figure 2.9. Now you should have a histogram like the one in Figure 2.1.

Figure 2.7: Format Data Series

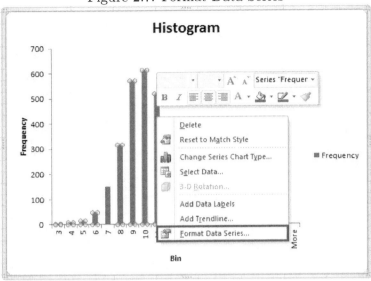

Figure 2.8: Gap Width

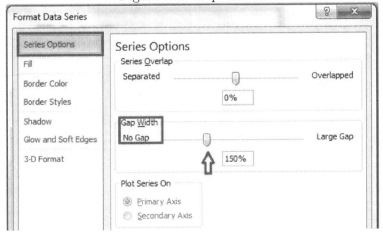

Figure 2.9: Border Color

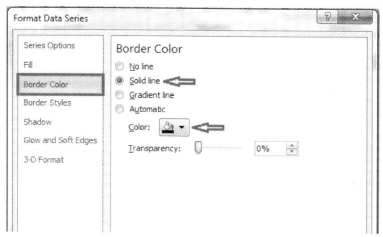

For a research project I did when in college I analyzed the distribution rate of obesity across the United States. I obtained the raw data from the Centers for Disease Control and Prevention website. One of the first steps in analyzing data is to produce a histogram. A histogram can tell you a lot about your data. Calculating descriptive statistics is the second step to analyzing data, which compliments your histogram. Descriptive statistics will be covered in a Chapter 3. For now, let us try to duplicate the histogram as seen in Figure 2.10.

Figure 2.10: Distribution of obese patients, 2008

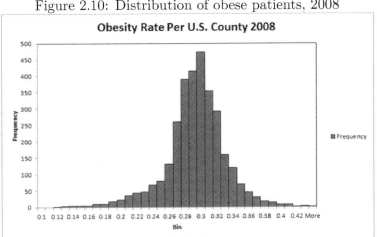

You can download this file titled **Obesity 2008** from `histogramma.`
`com` under **Data** and create a histogram from it. Let's go through it.

- Calculate the maximum and minimum values of the data set. This
  determines the range of your data, hence evaluating the bin size.

- Click the **Data** tab.

- Click the **Data Analysis** button.

- Look for **Histogram** and click **OK**.

- Enter **A1:A3141** in the **Input Range** text box or by selecting
  the cells using the mouse.

- Enter the bin range cells **B1:B34** in the **Bin Range** text box.

- Select **Chart Output**.

- Click **OK**.

The histogram is complete at this point but let's make it look better.

- Right-click on one of the blue data series bars.

- Select **Format Data Series**.

- In the dialogue box, select **Series Options**.

- Toggle the **Gap Width** slide button to the left for 0% gap.

- Select the **Border Color** button.

- Select the **Solid line** radio button.

- Select the **Color** of your choice.

There you have it! You just created a histogram.

Of course, you can play around with the size of the histogram chart simply by clicking the lower-right corner and stretching it. You can also change the heading, legend, colors, styles, etc. See figure 2.8 on how you can change the style of the histogram.

Figure 2.11: Styling options

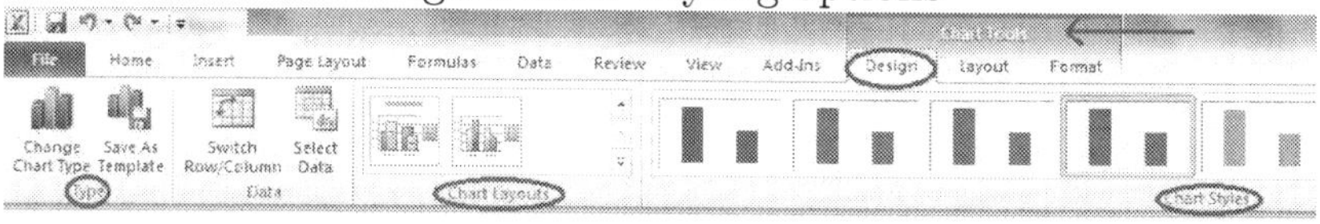

Select the **Chart Tools** tab first, then select **Change Chart Type** and browse which chart type best suits your needs. You can then select a chart layout from **Chart Layouts** and a chart style from **Chart Styles**.

Chapter 3

Descriptive Statistics

What is descriptive statistics? What does it tell us? Descriptive statistics are useful if you are not going to predict a result to any larger group. If you were to predict a result then that is referred to as inferential statistics rather than descriptive statistics. This would mean you are making predictions or *inferences* about a population from your analysis. Descriptive statistics includes statistical procedures that we use to describe the population we are trying to study. The data could be collected from either a sample or a population. Measures of central tendency, which are used in descriptive statistics, include the mean, median and mode, which was discussed in Chapter 1. Measures of variability include the standard deviation, the minimum and maximum variables, kurtosis, and skewness. These will be discussed in this chapter.

3.1 Standard Deviation and Variance

Once you find the mean of your data set you can calculate the standard deviation, but what is standard deviation? It essentially tells you how spread out numbers are from the mean. If the data are more spread out then the larger the deviation. The more clustered they are the smaller the deviation. It is important to note that there is a slight difference from calculating the standard deviation for a *sample* and *population*. If your data consists of a sample from a population, say, the heights of a few randomly selected students attending a university then you would use the *Sample Standard Deviation* formula. If, for example, you were to analyze the heights of *all* the students in your psychology class then you would use the *Population Standard Deviation* formula.

You can calculate the sample standard deviation using the formula

$$s = \sqrt{\frac{\sum (x_i - \bar{x})^2}{n - 1}}$$

This formula looks intimidating but don't be alarmed. s is the standard deviation, x_i represents each individual data point in your set, $\bar{x}$ is the mean of your sample data, and n is the number of data points you have. To calculate the population standard deviation we use the formula

$$\sigma = \sqrt{\frac{\sum (x_i - \mu)^2}{n}}$$

Again, don't be alarmed. σ is the Greek symbol sigma which represents the standard deviation of the entire *population*, μ is the Greek symbol mu which represents the mean of the population, x_i still represents each individual data point in your set and n is still the number of data points you have. It is important to distinguish these symbols.

There has been argument about the use of n and $n - 1$. Some top statisticians argue that there really is no significance in n vs. $n - 1$. You can check out the views of Terence P. Speed, a top biostatistician, by visiting **http://bulletin.imstat.org/2012/12/terences-stuff-n-vs-n-1/** to read more about it. Also, you will see that Excel produces slightly different answers due to using slightly different formulas, but there is really no need to worry about a small difference in results.

Let us take a minute to look at a very small example just so we can get a sense of standard deviations. Suppose we randomly took measurements of the heights of a few students–to keep things simple–say, thirty, at a university. Their heights, in inches, measure as follows:

$$\{69, 69, 64, 68, 65, 69, 70, 59, 60, 64, 63, 62, 67, 61, 66,$$
$$67, 73, 65, 63, 73, 64, 70, 67, 67, 71, 65, 60, 69, 79, 65\}$$

The first step we take is to calculate the mean of the heights. The mean is 66 inches. The next step is to subtract the mean from each data point in the set.

69-66=3	70-66=4	67-66=1	63-66=-3	71-66=5
69-66=3	59-66=-7	61-66=-5	73-66=7	65-66=-1
64-66=-2	60-66=-6	66-66=0	64-66=-2	60-66=-6
68-66=2	64-66=-2	67-66=1	70-66=4	69-66=3
65-66=-1	63-66=-3	73-66=7	67-66=1	79-66=13
69-66=3	62-66=-4	65-66=-1	67-66=1	65-66=-1

Next, square each of these values

$3^2 = 9$	$4^2 = 16$	$1^2 = 1$	$(-3)^2 = 9$	$5^2 = 25$
$3^2 = 9$	$(-7)^2 = 49$	$(-5)^2 = 25$	$7^2 = 49$	$(-1)^2 = 1$
$(-2)^2 = 4$	$(-6)^2 = 36$	$0^2 = 0$	$(-2)^2 = 4$	$(-6)^2 = 36$
$2^2 = 4$	$(-2)^2 = 4$	$1^2 = 1$	$4^2 = 16$	$3^2 = 9$
$(-1)^2 = 1$	$(-3)^2 = 9$	$7^2 = 49$	$1^2 = 1$	$13^2 = 169$
$3^2 = 9$	$(-4)^2 = 16$	$(-1)^2 = 1$	$1^2 = 1$	$(-1)^2 = 1$

Now add up each of the squared values

$$9 + 9 + 4 + 4 + 1 + 9 + 16 + 49 + 36 + 4 + 9 + 16 + 1 + 25 + 0+$$
$$1 + 49 + 1 + 9 + 49 + 4 + 16 + 1 + 1 + 25 + 1 + 36 + 9 + 169 + 1 = 564$$

Next, divide 564 by n-1, where n-1=30-1=29, so

$$\frac{564}{n-1} = \frac{564}{30-1} = \frac{564}{29} = 19.4$$

and, finally, take the square root of 19.4

$$\sqrt{19.4} = 4.41$$

What do we do with this number? If we add and subtract 4.41 to/from the mean, 66, we will have one standard deviation from the mean. If the height data follows a bell-shaped distribution, commonly known as a normal distribution, then it means that approximately 68% of the population will fall between the heights of $66 - 4.41 = 61.6$ and $66 + 4.41 = 70.4$ inches. Let's look at this in a graphical sense.

Figure 3.1: Normal Distribution Curve

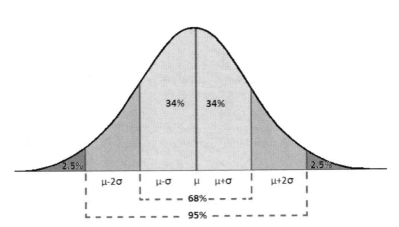

histogramma.com

The figure above shows how a normal distribution curve looks. The red center line is the mean of the data, μ. Within one standard deviation, that is, $\mu + \sigma$, (34%), and $\mu - \sigma$, (34%), from the mean represents about 68% of the data. Two standard deviations, $\mu + 2\sigma$ and $\mu - 2\sigma$, from the mean represents about 95% of the data.

Remember the number 19.4 we got from calculating the standard deviation just before we took the square root? Well, that number is the **variance**. What is variance? Variance is the average of the squared deviations from the mean. It is simply finding the mean of your data, subtracting the mean from each data point, squaring each of those values and dividing by $n - 1$ or n, depending if you have a sample of a population or the whole population. So, the variance is 19.4 and the standard deviation is the square root of the variance, which is 4.41. What this means is that, on average, the thirty students are about 19.4 inches apart in height.

Sample Standard Deviation	Population Standard Deviation
$s = \sqrt{\frac{\sum(x_i - \bar{x})^2}{n-1}}$	$\sigma = \sqrt{\frac{\sum(x_i - \mu)^2}{n}}$

Now that you have an idea on how to calculate the variance and standard deviation by hand let's calculate the variance and standard deviation for the previous example using Excel. If you had not already done so, enter the thirty data points into Excel from the previous example of student heights, or you may download the file from `histogramma.com` under **Data** titled **Student Heights**.

Select all the cells, **A1:A30**, to calculate the mean. The mean should now appear in **A31** as 66.46667. Round this number down to 66. Next, subtract the mean from each data entry. In cell **B1**, enter **=A1-66**, hit **Enter**. Click **B1** once and hover the mouse over the bottom-right corner until you see the bold cross. Click, hold and drag down to the last data entry, **B30**.

You then need to square these differences. In cell **C1** enter

`=B1^2`

and as before hover the mouse to select the bold cross to drag down to the last data entry, **C30**.

Now sum up the **C** column, **C1:C30**, which should sum up to 564. In **D1** enter **=564/29**. Remember, we divide by 29 because we are sampling (30 students) from a population (all students at the university). Finally we take the square root of **D1**, 19.4, which is equal to about 4.41.

The run-down:

$$n = \text{number of students} = 30$$
$$\bar{x} = \text{mean} = 66$$
$$s^2 = \text{variance} = 19.4$$
$$s = \text{standard deviation} = 4.41$$

There is a simpler way to calculate the variance and standard deviation with Excel. The use of **VAR.S** and **STDEV.S** can help this situation. Type in **VAR.S(A1:A30)** in cell **E1** and then hit **ENTER**. Enter **STDEV.S(A1:A30)** in cell **E2** and then hit **ENTER**. You will notice that there is a slight difference for variance and standard deviation. Excel is using a slightly different formula, as mentioned earlier, but I would not worry too much about it. Use **VAR.P** and **STDEV.P** if you are calculating from a population.

3.2   Minimum and Maximum Variables

Minimum and maximum variables are simple. If you have a set of numbers, say, {2,5,7,11,12,15,19,20,21,33}, then it can easily be seen that 2 is the minimum value and 33 is the maximum value. You could have a sample of 1,500 data points and may or may not be numerically ordered. Of course, in dealing with very large data sets you would want Excel to evaluate these figures. This topic was briefly discussed in Chapter 2 but it is worth going over it again.

Minimum:

- Enter =**MIN(** in a blank cell.

- Select the range of your data by highlighting the cell range or by typing in the parameters (cell range i.e. A1:A462).

- Type **)** to close the argument and press **Enter**.

Maximum:

- Enter =**MAX(** in a blank cell.

- Select the range of your data by highlighting the cell range or by typing in the parameters (cell range i.e. A1:A462).

- Type **)** to close the argument and press **Enter**.

The **range** of a data set is simply the difference between the largest value minus the smallest value.

Range = largest value − smallest value.

The range for our small example is 31. Range = 33 − 2 = 31. What is the range used for? What does it tell you? The range will tell you the spread of the data set. If the range is small then that indicates that the values of the set are bunched together. If the range is large then it indicates that the values of the data set are dispersed. If you are taking a survey for a particular group of people for a medical condition you may want to know the range of their age. Such an example would be ages 18-25 for a sleep study, or an activity rate for ages 50+. Maybe you want to know what the dispersion, range, is for students who graduated in a particular field of study. How do we calculate the range in Excel? It can be done a couple of ways. Here's how.

Range:

- Find the minimum and maximum values of your data set as done in the above procedure.

- In a blank cell enter **=B2-B1** assuming you calculated the minimum value and maximum value in cells B1 and B2, respectively.

- Press **Enter**.

or

- Enter **=Max(A1:A10) - Min(A1:A10)** in a blank cell, assuming your data is in this cell range.

- Press **Enter**.

You can practice this using the example data sets provided in chapters 1 and 2.

3.3 Standard Score

What is the standard score? What does it tell us? The standard score, or z-score, gives the number of standard deviations between the

measurement and the mean of the distribution. It is obtained by subtracting the population mean μ from an individual raw score x and then
dividing the difference by the population standard deviation σ.

$$z = \frac{x - \mu}{\sigma}$$

They can also tell us how far a particular score is away from the mean.
A positive z-score is above the mean; negative is below. A zero z-score
value is equal to the mean. Z-scores help us understand how typical a
particular score is within a bunch of scores. Approximately 95% of the
data should have Z-score between -2 and +2, if the data are normally
distributed. If z-scores fall outside this range they may be considered
outliers of the data. Let's look at this grapically.

Figure 3.2: Z-score, Normal Distribution Curve

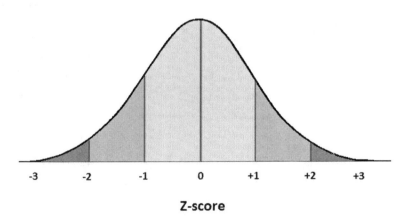

Z-score

histogramma.com

Notice the positive z-scores are to the right, or above the mean and
the negative z-scores are to the left, or below the mean.

We can actually go ahead and calculate the z-scores for the obesity example from chapter 2. First we need to calculate the mean and
standard deviation of the data set. Lastly, we subtract the mean from
each individual data point and divide that difference by the standard

deviation. You should have obtained $\mu = 10.0$ and $\sigma = 2.14$. Now, to calculate the z-score you should enter the following:

- Enter =(A2-B2)/B3, assuming B2 is the mean and B3 is the standard deviation.

- Copy down to A3220.

There you have it! You just calculated the z-scores for the data set. You may also want to sort these z-scores in ascending order so you can actually see the negative and positive tail-ends of the distribution.

3.4 Skewness

What is skewness? Skewness is a measure of how much data is concentrated above or below the mean. Data can be skewed left or right. Skewed left values are negative, skewed right values are positive, and a non-skewed distribution will have a value of zero. The concept of skewness is quite simple, though can seem complex at first glance. Let us look at it this way: We now know the z-score is calculated using the formula

$$z = \frac{x - \mu}{\sigma}.$$

If we replace x with μ, and E is the expected value, we then have

$$E\left(\frac{\mu - \mu}{\sigma}\right) = E\left(\frac{0}{\sigma}\right)$$
$$= 0$$

This makes sense if you think about it because the mean is zero deviations from itself. If we square the z-score

$$\frac{x - \mu}{\sigma}$$

to get

$$\left(\frac{x-\mu}{\sigma}\right)^2$$

then calculate its average, we get

$$E\left(\left(\frac{x-\mu}{\sigma}\right)^2\right) = \frac{1}{\sigma^2}E\left((x-\mu)^2\right)$$
$$= \frac{\sigma^2}{\sigma^2}$$
$$= 1$$

So, calculating the average of the z-score and the square of the z-score does not tell us anything new. However, calculating the cube,

$$\left(\frac{x-\mu}{\sigma}\right)^3,$$

of the z-score tells us a lot about the distribution of the data about the mean. If the z-score is bigger than 1 then its cube, z^3, will be much bigger than 1. Similarly, if the z-score, z, is less than -1 then its cube, z^3, will be much more negative. On the other hand, if the z-score is between -1 and 1, then cube will be much smaller in size than z. So, z^3 will be positive or negative, accordingly. The average value

$$\left(\frac{x-\mu}{\sigma}\right)^3$$

of z^3 is called the *skewness* of the data. To better understand this let us look at a couple of examples.

If we take the student heights data we can calculate the skewness by the z-score. First, calculate the mean and population standard deviation in cells B1 and B2, respectively. In cell C1, type in $=$**(A1-\$B\$1)/\$B\$2** to calculate the z-score. Drag the formula down to C30 by selecting C1 and hovering the mouse pointer over the bottom-right corner. Sort this column in ascending order. In C31, calculate the average of z-scores from C1 through C30. You should get 0. In D1, type in $=C1^2$, using **SHIFT + 6** to get the 2 above the 1, and copy down this formula to D30. Sort this column in ascending order. Calculate the average of these in D31. In this cell you should get 1.

Note: you may need to adjust the number of decimal places in these cells to get 0 and 1. You can do this by highlighting the column of interest, clicking to the **Home** tab, and then clicking the **Decrease Decimal** button until you get three decimal places of accuracy.

Finally, type in $=C1^3$ in cell E1 and copy down this formula to E30. Calculate the average of these in E31. In this cell you should get 0.594 which is the skewness.

Now try using the skew function in cell E32 by typing in **=SKEW(A1:A30)**. The result is 0.625. This isn't the same as our last result. Again, Excel uses a different formula. They use the formula

$$\frac{n}{(n-1)(n-2)} \sum \left(\frac{x_i - \mu}{s}\right)^3$$

for the skewness, this is a *slightly* different formula to the one we discussed, but is neither right nor wrong.

Figure 3.3 below is a distribution of the number of diabetes patients in 2005. Notice that the skewness is positive, 0.424, which is skewed right.

Figure 3.3: Diabetes patients, 2005

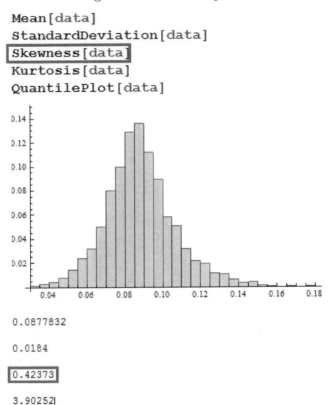

`Mean[data]`
`StandardDeviation[data]`
`Skewness[data]`
`Kurtosis[data]`
`QuantilePlot[data]`

0.0877832

0.0184

0.42373

3.90252|

In Figure 3.4 the distribution of obese patients in 2004 has a negative skewness, -0.370, which is skewed left.

Figure 3.4: Obese patients, 2004

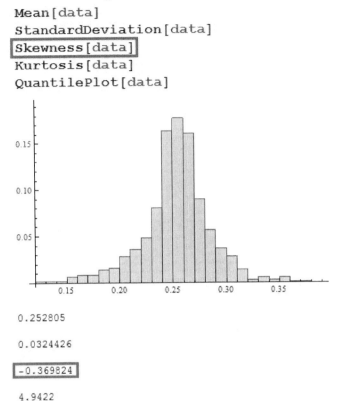

```
Mean[data]
StandardDeviation[data]
Skewness[data]
Kurtosis[data]
QuantilePlot[data]
```

```
0.252805

0.0324426

-0.369824

4.9422
```

Let's calculate the skewness in Excel using the example of student heights. In a blank cell type in **=SKEW(A1:A30)** and hit **ENTER**. You should get 0.625.

3.5 Kurtosis

What is kurtosis? Kurtosis is the measure of the "peakiness" of the distribution. A normal kurtosis will have a value of 3. Again, the concept of kurtosis is quite simple though can be complex at first glance. If we continue our discussion on z-scores from the last section we can determine the kurtosis. The z-score for z^4,

$$\left(\frac{x - \mu}{\sigma}\right)^4,$$

is much smaller than z when z is between -1 and 1, and much bigger when z is bigger than 1. Note that z^4 is always greater than or equal to 0, in other words, positive. The average value

$$\left(\frac{x - \mu}{\sigma}\right)^4$$

of z^4 is called the *kurtosis* of the data. To better understand this let us look at a couple of examples.

Continuing on with the student heights data from the previous section we can calculate the kurtosis. In cell F1 type in =$C1^4$ and copy down this formula to F30. In F31 type in =**AVERAGE(F1:F30)-3** to get 0.624 which is the kurtosis.

Now try using the kurtosis function in cell E32 by typing in =**KURT(A1:A30)**. The result is 0.972. This isn't the same as our last result. Again, Excel uses a different formula. They use the formula

$$\left[\frac{n(n + 1)}{(n - 1)(n - 2)(n - 3)} \sum \left(\frac{x_i - \mu}{s}\right)^4\right] - \frac{3(n - 1)^2}{(n - 2)(n - 3)}$$

for the kurtosis.

Figure 3.4 below is a distribution of the number of diabetes patients in 2005. Notice that the kurtosis is 3.90, which is approximately normal.

Figure 3.5: Diabetes patients, 2005

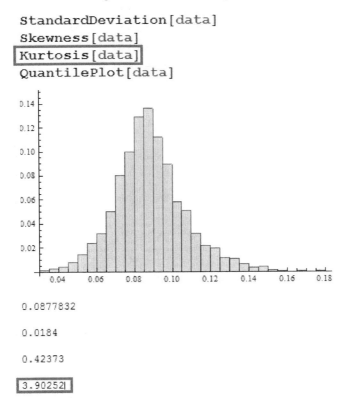

StandardDeviation[data]
Skewness[data]
Kurtosis[data]
QuantilePlot[data]

0.0877832

0.0184

0.42373

3.90252

In Figure 3.5 the kurtosis for the distribution of obese patients in 2004 is 4.94.

Figure 3.6: Obese patients, 2004

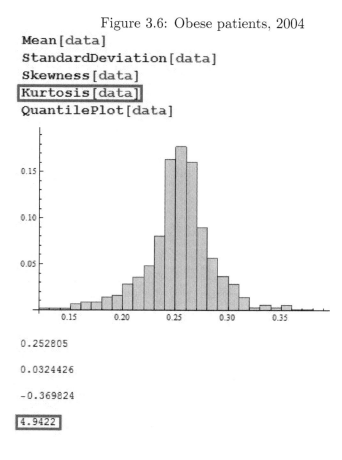

```
Mean[data]
StandardDeviation[data]
Skewness[data]
Kurtosis[data]
QuantilePlot[data]
```

0.252805

0.0324426

-0.369824

4.9422

Let's calculate the kurtosis using Excel, again, using the example of student heights. In a blank cell type in **=KURT(A1:A30)** and hit **ENTER**. You should get 0.972. Real easy!

3.6   Summary Statistics

In the previous chapters and sections I have shown you how to calculate several basic and advanced summary statistics. Now, you don't have to calculate each of these statistics individually; Excel can output all of these, and more, summary statistics at once. I have shown you how to do each one individually so that you can learn how each is calculated by hand and/or with Excel. Your most basic descriptive statistics will become easier once you learn how to obtain them all at once.

Let's replicate the diabetes patients example from Figure 3.4 by first downloading the Excel spreadsheet file from `histogramma.com` under **Data** title **Diabetes 2005**.

From here perform the steps necessary to produce a histogram. Now to get the summary statistics click on **Data** then **Data Analysis**, refer to figures 3.6 and 3.7. The Data Analysis dialogue box will appear. Select **Descriptive Statistics** then click **OK** as shown in Figure 3.8. A new dialogue box will appear (Figure 3.9). In the **Input Range** textbox enter **A2:A3220**. In the **Output Range** textbox enter **B2**, or whichever cell you want. Lastly, click on the **Summary Statistics** checkbox. Click **OK**. Now you should have the same results as in Figure 3.10.

Figure 3.7: Click Data tab

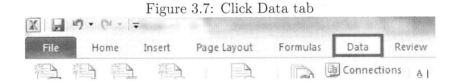

Figure 3.8: Click Data Analysis

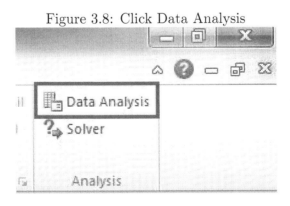

Figure 3.9: Click Descriptive Statistics

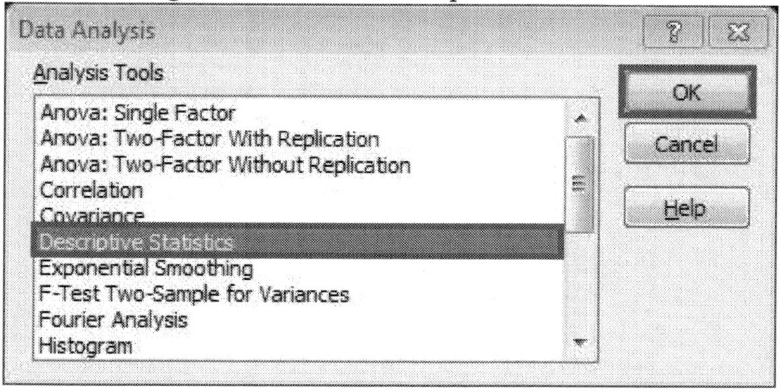

Figure 3.10: Enter information

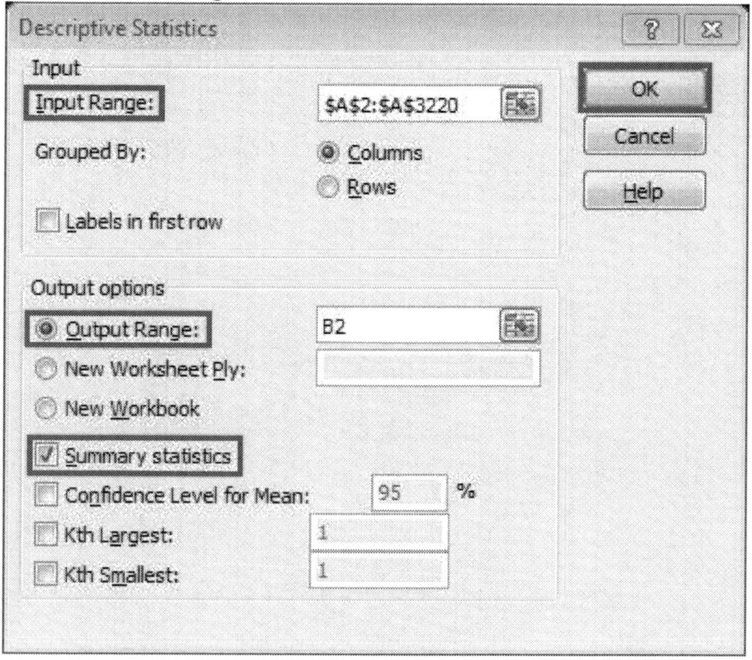

Figure 3.11: Complete summary statistics

	A	B	C	D
1	**Percent**			
2	10.9	*Column1*		
3	14.9			
4	14.6	Mean	8.738459	
5	12.9	Standard E	0.032454	
6	13.6	Median	8.6	
7	13.8	Mode	8.6	
8	14.5	Standard E	1.84134	
9	13.9	Sample Vä	3.390534	
10	13.9	Kurtosis	0.896826	
11	12.9	Skewness	0.44161	
12	11	Range	14.7	
13	11.4	Minimum	3	
14	13	Maximum	17.7	
15	11.7	Sum	28129.1	
16	12.1	Count	3219	
17	12			
18	12.4			

As you can see it is very easy to produce the summary statistics all at once in comparison to calculating each one individually. Download **Diabetes 2006** from `histogramma.com` to get more practice. Let's go through it.

- Produce the histogram for this data.

- Click on the **Data** tab then **Data Analysis** button.

- Select **Descriptive Statistics** then click **OK**.

- Enter **A2:A3220** in the **Input Range** textbox.

- Enter a cell in **Output Range** textbox.

- Click on the **Summary Statistics** checkbox.

- Click **OK**.

There you have it! You should have the following results:

Mean	...	9.3
Standard Error	...	0.036
Median	...	9.1
Mode	...	9
Standard Deviation	...	2.02
Sample Variance	...	4.10
Kurtosis	...	0.401
Skewness	...	0.380
Range	...	14.4
Minimum	...	3.1
Maximum	...	17.5
Sum	...	29934.5
Count	...	3219

Figure 3.12: Histogram of diabetes patients, 2006

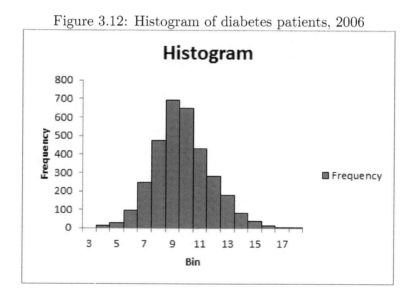

Chapter 4

Creating Pivot Charts

Pivot-charts are very common in analyzing the frequency of categorical items. Such examples would include what people drive, person's favorite sport, how many hours of television is watched per week, etc. The data can come from a poll, survey, business records, medical records, etc. A pivot-chart can automatically count, sort, total or even calculate the average of the data.

To begin a pivot-chart we need, of course, some data. Let's take a look at a small sample of data collected from a survey of 35 people at random. The survey question was, "Which computer operating system do you currently use?" There were only two answers to choose from: Mac or Windows. Each answer was entered into an Excel spreadsheet. To obtain this data, titled **Software**, go to `histogramma.com` under **Data**.

Now that you have the data let's create a pivot-chart. It is important to have a title, though not necessary. In doing so, it helps to keep data neat and organized (see figure 4.1).

Figure 4.1: Column A with header

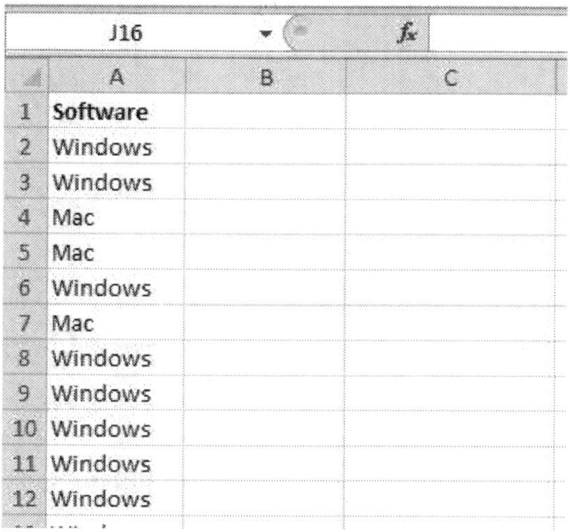

	A	B	C
J16		f_x	
1	**Software**		
2	Windows		
3	Windows		
4	Mac		
5	Mac		
6	Windows		
7	Mac		
8	Windows		
9	Windows		
10	Windows		
11	Windows		
12	Windows		

First click on a blank cell, preferably somewhere in the upper C column, say **C2**. Then click the **Insert** tab, click **PivotTable** and select **PivotChart**. A dialogue box will appear on your screen. Where it says **Table/Range** enter the cells in which the data occurs; **A1:A36**. Or you can select the cells with your mouse pointer containing the cells **A1** through **A36**. This includes the header '**Software**'! You can then select whether you want the pivot-chart to appear on the existing worksheet or on another worksheet. To keep things a little simpler I have chosen to place the pivot-chart on the existing worksheet. Click **OK**. Refer to Figures 4.2 and 4.3.

Figure 4.2: Insert, PivotTable, PivotChart

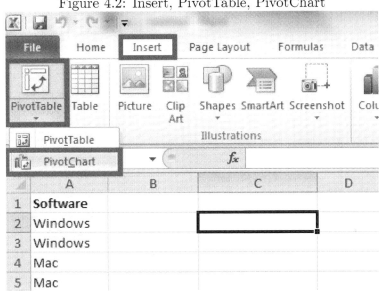

Figure 4.3: Enter data in Table/Range

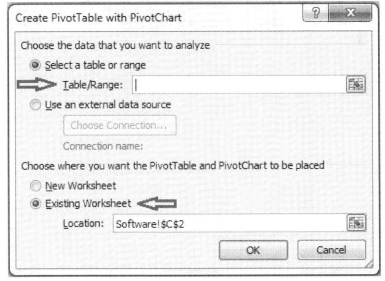

Now your worksheet should look similar to figure 4.4 with minor and irrelevant differences depending on where you placed your pivot-chart via clicking on a blank cell other than where I have placed mine in this exercise.

Figure 4.4: PivotTable and PivotChart

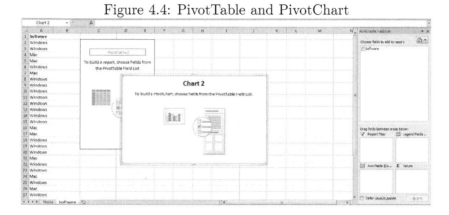

You should notice on the far-right window titled **PivotTable Field List** the header **Software**. Excel recognizes the header and its contents when you select all the cells for the pivot-chart as you had done earlier. Drag and drop 'Software' to **Axis Fields** and to **Values**.

Figure 4.5: Drag and drop 'Software' to Axis Fields and Values

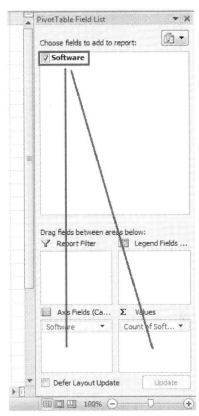

Once you drag and drop you will automatically see the pivot-table and pivot-chart appear (Figure 4.6). From here you can edit the colors and styling of your newly developed pivot-chart and also the chart title and legend (refer to Figure 2.7 on how to style the pivot-chart).

Figure 4.6: Pivot-table and pivot-chart

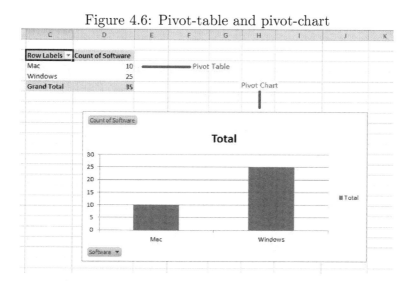

If you want to control the categories from the pivot-chart you can. Click on the **Software** button from the chart (Figure 4.7), then select either **Mac** or **Windows** (Figure 4.8) to display it. You can always go back to view both by selecting **Select All**.

Figure 4.7: Select category

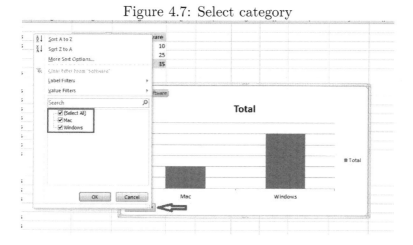

Figure 4.8: Mac or Windows selection

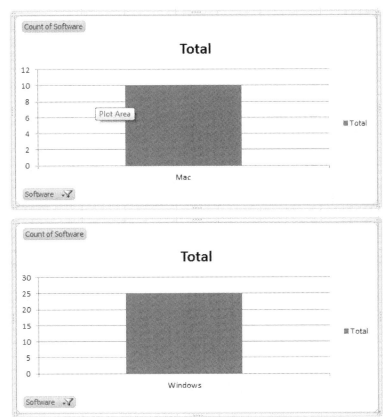

Let's try something a little different with the functionality of the pivot-chart. Drag and drop **Software** from **Axis Fields** to **Legend Fields**. You now get a side-by-side color-coded display. Try it and you should get something like in Figure 4.9.

Figure 4.9: Legend Fields

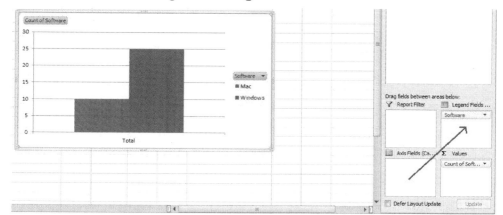

I wanted to analyze the distribution of vehicles that are on the road in the city that I live in. I took a sheet of paper attached to a clipboard and sat on the porch outside of my house. On the sheet of paper I documented every vehicle that passed by. In the process I excluded motorcycles and commercial vehicles mainly because I only wanted to see what people drive on a daily basis. 400 entries were documented with 31 different vehicle makes. This is a good example for distribution of vehicle makes so let's create a pivot-chart for it. See figure 4.10.

Figure 4.10: Vehicle make distribution

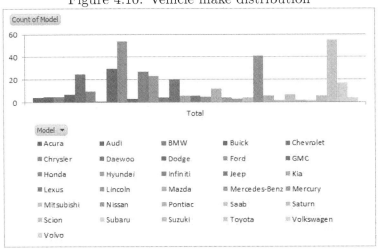

You can download this file titled **Vehicle Make** from `histogramma.com` under **Data** and create a pivot-chart from it. Let's go through it.

- Click on a blank cell to the right of the list of vehicle makes to where you want the pivot-table positioned. The pivot-chart can be positioned wherever you like by dragging it around.

- Click the **Insert** tab, click **PivotTable** and select **PivotChart**.

- In the dialogue box enter the cells in which the data occurs into the textbox where it says Table/Range. Don't forget to include the header.

- Select whether you want the pivot-chart to appear on the existing worksheet or on another work-sheet. Click **OK**.

- Drag and drop 'Model' to **Axis Fields** and to **Legend Fields**.

- Double-click on the legend box, but not on an individual legend, and a dialogue box will appear titled **Format Legend**.

- Select **Bottom** then click **Close**.

There you have it! You just created a pivot chart on your own.

Chapter 5

Importing Data Into Excel

Sometimes the most difficult part of statistics is extracting data. They can be documented in sources other than an Excel spreadsheet. There are times when you want to download data from a text file or even from the web. There are a number of ways to import data into Excel. This chapter will cover how to extract data from various sources.

5.1   Text Files

So you know how to download Excel files right off the Internet since you have done so for the previous examples, but what if those files were text files? What if someone supplied you with a text file via a USB drive, or another device? How would you get data from that? It is simpler than you think.

From `histogramma.com` under **Data**, click **Diabetes 2004** to download to your computer. A new tab will open in your browser as a text read-out. Use combination keys **CTRL** and **A**, (**CTRL + A**), to select all the data on that page. Next, open up MS Notepad to paste in the text. Save the text file as "Diabetes 2004". (You can actually extract this raw data by following the steps in section 5.3 without going through this trouble, but realistically it is another technique for digging up data.) Suppose this file was sitting in your computer or was from a USB drive, which makes no difference, you can import this data from Excel.

With Excel open, click the **Data** tab and click the **From Text** button. Find and select **Diabetes 2004** to import it. A new dialogue box will appear that consists of three steps to follow. Keep clicking **Next** until the third step and click **Finish**. A new dialogue box will appear prompting for the location of the data to be placed, in other words, which cell do you want to place the data in. For simplicity select the default cell, A1. Click **OK** and your data will appear in Excel (refer to figures 5.1-5.5).

Figure 5.1: Data from text

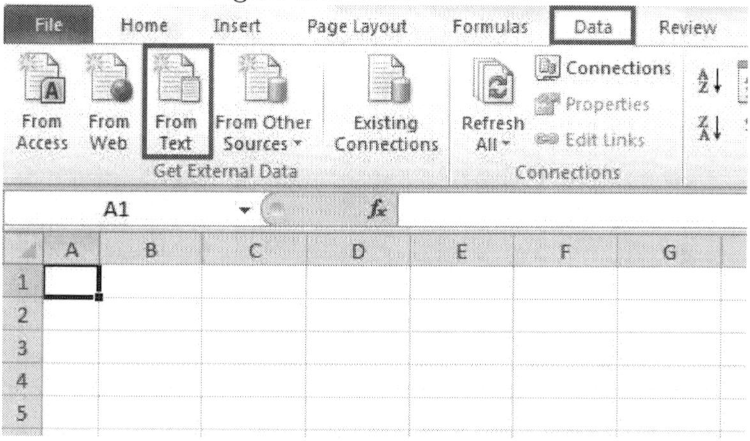

Figure 5.2: Text Import Wizard, step 1 of 3

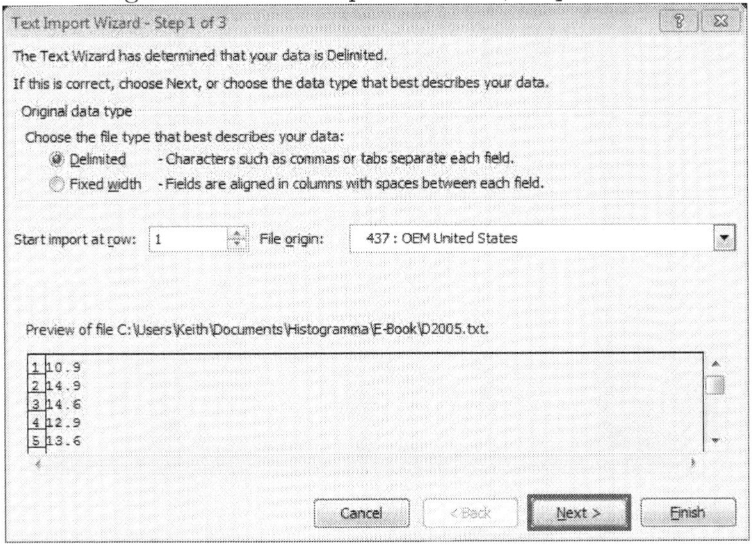

Figure 5.3: Text Import Wizard, step 2 of 3

Figure 5.4: Text Import Wizard, step 3 of 3

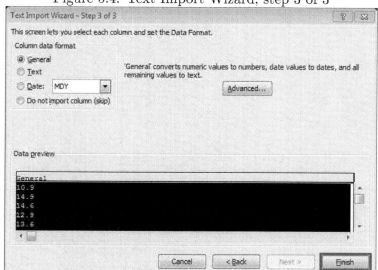

Figure 5.5: Import data

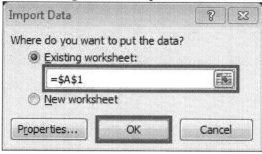

Let's try another example of extracting data from a text file. Download **Diabetes 2007** from `histogramma.com` under **Data**. The steps are similar as before.

- Open up Excel and click on the **Data** tab.

- Click on the **From Text** button.

- Find and select **Diabetes 2007**, click **Import**.

- Click **Next** until the third step and click **Finish**.

- Select a cell you wish to place your data.

- Click **OK**.

There you have it! You imported data to Excel from a text file.

5.2 CSV Files

What is a CSV file? It stands for comma-separated values. It is mainly simple text separated by commas, hence its name, or by semicolons and tabs.

If you go to imf.org, you will notice that you can directly download CSV files straight to your computer and it will open up in Excel. There is really nothing to it. Click on the file and Excel will open up. Now you have access to the data for you to analyze.

Also, if you have CSV files on your computer the steps for importing data to Excel is very simple. Double-click on the CSV file and it will open in Excel automatically. It is similar to clicking the CSV file from the link above.

5.3 Web Files

There are times when you will come across a set of data on the web that you would like to download but can't because there is no link for it. What do you do then? Do you sit there and enter each item into Excel? No. There is a simpler way and Excel can do it.

Suppose you wanted the table from the Bureau of Labor Statistics shown in Figure 5.6. How can we put this table into Excel? If you already haven't done so, open up Excel and click on the **Data** tab and click on the **From Web** button. Once you click on this button a browser will pop. In this browser enter the exact address of the data you want to download: http://www.bls.gov/cps/cpsaat01.htm. Note: You may be on the web prior to these steps but Excel will open a browser for you and you must enter the address in that browser. Click **Go** for the page to appear and then click **Import**. A new dialogue box will appear prompting for the location of the data to be placed. For simplicity select the default cell, A1. Click **OK** and your data will appear in Excel (refer to figures 5.7-5.9). From here you may want to do a little clean up by deleting excess clutter to maintain only the data.

Figure 5.6: Table from the web

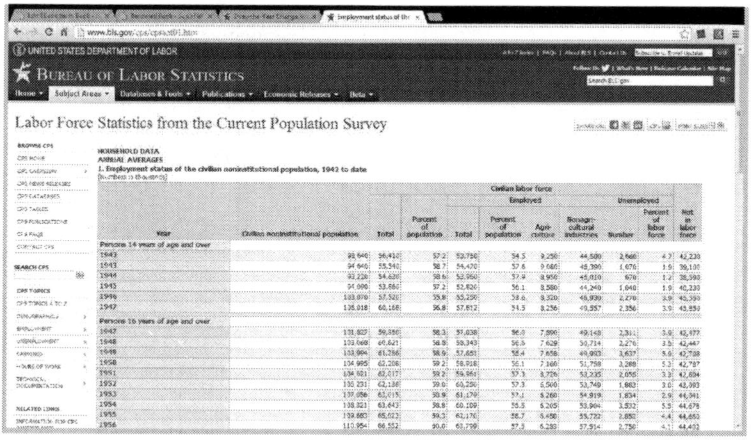

Figure 5.7: Data from the web

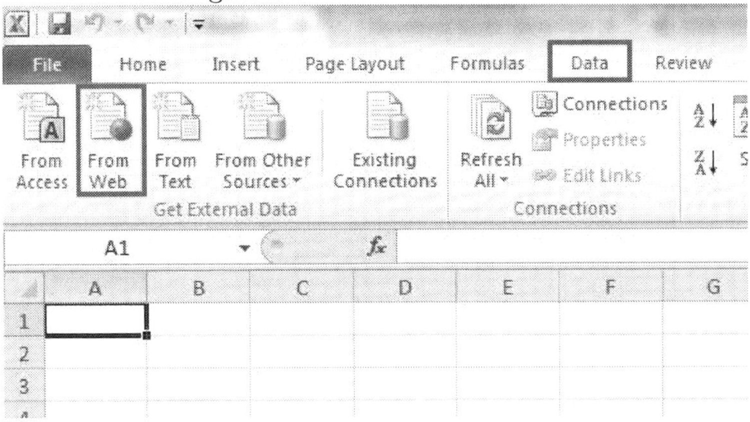

Figure 5.8: Web address dialogue box

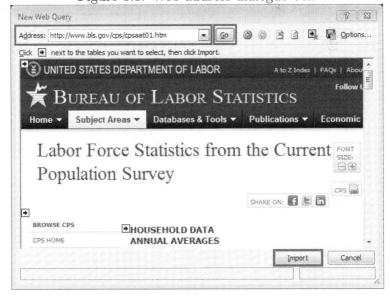

Figure 5.9: Import data

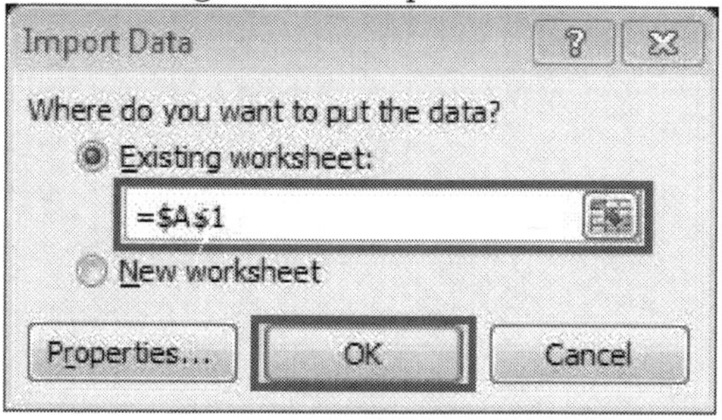

Let's try another example of extracting data from the web. Suppose you find a table on the web that you want to import to Excel as in Figure 5.6 from Bureau of Labor Statistics. The steps are similar as before.

- Open up Excel and click on the **Data** tab.

- Click on the **From Web** button.

- In the browser, enter the exact web address of the data.

- Click **Go**.

- Click **Import**.

- Select a cell you wish to place your data.

- Click **OK**.

There you have it! You imported data to Excel from the web.

5.4 Sorting Data

Many times when you get data it may not always be sorted. You may have data that needs to be in ascending order, or maybe descending order. What if you have data that is mixed with 'yes' and 'no' responses from a survey? What if you wanted to make two histograms with this data? Well, Excel can do this too. Using the sort command is very easy.

It is located near the top-right area of the menu bar. Different options are shown when you click **Sort & Filter**, and two of the most common options are **Sort A to Z** and **Sort Z to A**, if you are sorting alphabetic data, or **Sort Smallest to Largest** and **Sort Largest to Smallest**, if you are sorting numerical data. See Figure 5.10.

Figure 5.10: Sort & Filter

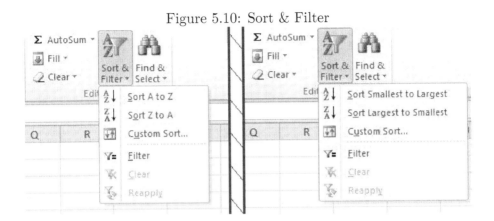

Let's try an example with a spreadsheet with some names. Download **Presidents** from `histogramma.com` and try to sort the names from A to Z. You will see that the spreadsheet consists of four columns titled "Order", "President", "Party", and "Re-elected". Suppose you want to sort the names in alphabetical order, how could this be done? It's simple. Highlight column B, which is the "President" column, click **Sort & Filter** and select **Sort A to Z**. Since there is data in columns A, C, and D Excel will prompt a dialogue box asking if you want to 'expand' or 'continue' with the sorting. This means that you have the choice to sort the column as is while the other two columns are not affected, or expand the selection so that the other data can "follow" the data that is tied to it. In this example I will expand the selection so that I can sort the presidents back to the order in which they were elected. If you don't have data that you do not wish to trace back or are needed to support it then you can just use the 'continue' option.

We can use the Sort & Filter command to do more complex sorting. Let's sort the data by 'Re-elected' and 'President' at the same time.

Sorting both categories simultaneously will allow us to list all presidents in alphabetical order to which they were re-elected.

First, highlight columns A through D. Click **Sort & Filter** and select **Custom Sort**. From here select 'Re-elected' from the drop-down menu that is to the right of 'Sort by'. Click the **Add Level** button to add another level of sorting, 'Then by'. Under this drop-down menu select 'President'. Click **OK**. Now you have the data sorted by re-election with the presidents listed alphabetically. Refer to Figures 5.11 and 5.12.

Figure 5.11: Sort & Filter, Custom Sort

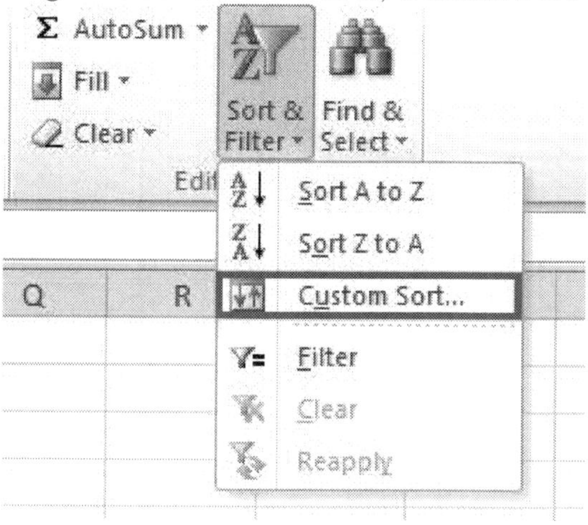

Figure 5.12: Sorting options

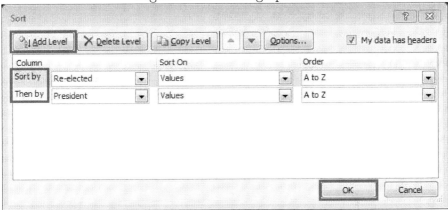

The sorting tool is very useful for data analyzing. You can use it for various purposes.

Exercises

1. What is the average, or mean, for the following sets? Median? Mode?

   (a) $\{5, 4, 12, 2, 1, 6, 5, 10, 20, 5, 10, 6, 11, 7\}$

   (b) $\{19, 11, 13, 5, 12, 1, 4, 6, 18, 10, 12, 9, 3, 7, 20\}$

   (c) $\{10, 16, 5, 15, 19, 6, 8, 20, 19, 14, 12, 17, 11, 13, 19, 18\}$

   (d) $\{19, 6, 9, 17, 7, 10, 11, 15, 2, 14, 16, 7, 12, 3, 8\}$

2. Calculate the standard deviation and variance for a, b, c, and d.

3. Using the information from questions 1 and 2 calculate the z-scores for a, b, c, and d.

4. Suppose a biologist records the length, in centimeters, for a sample of fish at four different ponds and she determines the mean and standard deviation for each, find the z-scores using the following parameters where $\bar{x}$ is the sample mean, s is the standard deviation, and x_i is a fish picked at random.

   (a) $\bar{x} = 46.9$, $s = 11.9$, $x_i = 63.0$

   (b) $\bar{x} = 59.1$, $s = 14.8$, $x_i = 70.0$

   (c) $\bar{x} = 10.4$, $s = 1.2$, $x_i = 12.0$

   (d) $\bar{x} = 7.6$, $s = 1.3$, $x_i = 11.1$

5. Download **Obesity 2004** from `histogramma.com`. Calculate the mean, median, and mode as done in Chapter 1. Calculate the population standard deviation and population variance.

6. Using the data from Obesity 2004, generate the summary statistics as done in Chapter 3, then make a histogram. Is the distribution skewed left or right?

7. Create a pivot chart for a topic of your choice where there are several categories and for each one there is a tally count. Think of the 'Vehicle Make' and 'Software' examples.

8. Sort the data in 'Vehicle Make' so that the data is sorted from largest to smallest.

9. Go to `histogramma.com` and click the "Birth Weight" link. Using the techniques from this book, download the data from the webpage, sort the data by smokers and nonsmokers, calculate the summary statistics for both smokers and nonsmokers, and create a histogram for each.

Index

About the Author

Keith Resendes currently resides in Fall River, Massachusetts, where he maintains and operates Histogramma^{TM}, a web-based statistical consulting and educational business. Keith received his B.A. in Mathematics from the University of Massachusetts in Dartmouth in the Fall of 2012, and has since founded Histogramma^{TM} to expand his passion for data analysis and statistical education. Through a network of professionals, Keith has extensive contacts in the statistical and data analysis fields. He also works on statistics education for beginners in data analysis. Please contact Keith for your data analysis and statistics education needs.

Follow Histogramma^{TM} on Twitter @histogramma1.
Like Histogramma^{TM} on Facebook.